Culture & Leisure Services
Red Doles Lane
Huddersfield, West Yorks. HD2 1YF

THIS BOOK SHOULD BE RETURNED ON OR BEFORE THE LATEST DATE STAMPED BELOW.
FINES ARE CHARGED IF THE ITEM IS LATE.

Getting through Depression with CBT:
A young person's guide

By Dr Louise Dalton & Dr Alice Farrington

Series Editor: Dr Claudia Herbert

Contents

With thanks to Claire Holdaway, Nicola Connolly, Ben Gurney-Smith and to the young people who made comments on earlier drafts of this booklet

Introduction

Everyone has different moods and sometimes feels sad and down in the dumps. Sometimes the sad feelings hang around for a long time and it's difficult to get going, even with the things you used to enjoy. When the sad feelings don't go away and really get in the way of your life we call this depression.

In this booklet we'll talk about depression, and introduce some of the ideas you'll be working on with your therapist to get through depression using CBT. It is recommended that the introductory book, called 'Getting through it with CBT: A young person's guide to Cognitive Behavioural Therapy (CBT)' is used in conjunction with this book for an even better understanding.

What is depression?

People describe depression in many different ways. Depression shows up in our thoughts, feelings, body reactions and what we do. It can look like this list below. You might be surprised at how many things are part of depression; there may be other things you would add on to the list.

Thoughts

I'm no good
Things will never get better
There's no point anymore
I hate myself and my life
No one cares about me
It's all my fault
Other thoughts

Feelings

Low
Sad
Irritable
Angry
Guilty
Other feelings

Body reactions

Weighed down
Sick
Tired
Aches and pains
Other body reactions..........

Things we do (behaviour)

Find it hard to do anything, even things you used to enjoy
Feel like you are walking through treacle
Restless
Find it hard to concentrate
Hurt yourself
Want to be alone
Argue a lot
Cry
Sleep a lot or find it hard to get to sleep
Not eat or eat a lot
Other behaviour

Self Harm

Sometimes depression can make you feel so bad, you might have thoughts about not wanting to live anymore, or wanting to hurt yourself. If this happens, it is very important that you tell your parents, doctor, teacher or another adult you trust immediately. These thoughts can be quite common in depression, and the ideas in this booklet should help you start to get through it.

What causes depression?

Depression can be a reaction to many different things, including change, bullying, illness, stress, trauma, or the death of someone close to you. Depression can involve changes in the way the chemicals in your body work.

Whatever starts the depression, how you **think** and what you **do** can keep the depression going. CBT tackles depression by working on the way you think and do things – the next section explains what this is all about.

How thoughts, feelings and behaviours link up

CBT is based on the idea that how you **think** about things affects how you **feel** and what you **do**.

Let's look at these examples

Jessica worked really hard for a test, but still got low marks. She thought; "*I'm so stupid, I'll never be any good, I might as well give up trying*" . Her thoughts made her feel disappointed and hopeless. She then didn't bother doing her homework and did badly the next time she had a test. I guess this would make Jessica think she really **is** stupid and there's no point in trying.

Danielle worked hard for the test and did badly too. She thought *"That test was really unfair, I'll show them next time"*. These thoughts made her feel a bit annoyed. However, thinking and feeling this way meant she was more motivated to work hard. This makes it more likely Danielle will do better the next time and feel pleased with her results.

In this example, the same thing has happened to both Jessica and Danielle, but they have had very different thoughts about it. It is their thoughts that have made them feel and do different things.

This is the same for all our thoughts, feelings and behaviour. Having depressed thoughts, like 'I'm bad" and "No one cares for me", makes us feel sad and then we can't be bothered to do anything.

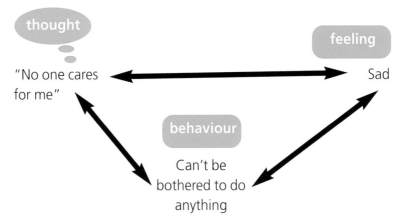

thought

"No one cares for me" ⟵⟶ Sad

feeling

Sad

behaviour

Can't be bothered to do anything

When our thoughts make us feel so sad that we stop doing things that we used to enjoy, or were good at, then we may end up thinking even worse thoughts about our lives. Depression changes the way we think about the world, so that it's as if you were looking through smudged glasses, making everything seem gloomy. This means we get trapped in a vicious cycle that keeps the depression going. It's a bit like being caught in a plughole, and it may feel very hard to escape.

What to expect from CBT

The good news is that there are ways to stop your life feeling like it's going down the drain. There are two important parts to this:

1. **Activity planning**. This involves what you do with your time.

2. **Sort your thoughts**. This involves catching your negative or spiky thoughts and seeing if there is a different way of looking at the situation.

These two strategies are part of CBT for depression, which helps people to break out of the vicious cycle that has been keeping the depression going.

You and your therapist will talk about what is **making** you feel sad and what is **keeping** you feeling sad. Your therapist will help you think about the way your thoughts, feelings and behaviour link up. Together you can draw a map of your problems. Then you can decide your goals and work out an escape plan. Your therapist will have worked with other people with similar problems, but remember you are the expert about your life.

You and your therapist will think about the two escape routes leading out of the depression – **what you do** and **how you think**. Together, you will work out tasks to try between the sessions, which will help you escape as quickly as possible. These will be things like keeping a diary of your activities, or catching and jotting down spiky thoughts (we'll talk about these a bit later on).

Activity planning

When our **thoughts** make us **feel** sad, it takes away our energy and enthusiasm to **do** things, not just schoolwork, but fun things too. If you stop doing things, then it gets harder and harder to do anything. Starting to **do** more again is a very important part of breaking out - if you're sitting in the bath and feel like you're going down the plughole, you need to get out of the bath!

Here are some reasons why activity planning helps:
* It may sound strange, but activity makes you feel less tired. The more you do, the more you feel like doing.
* Doing things takes your mind off your spiky thoughts
* Doing things makes you feel better about yourself
* Activity helps your brain keep sharp

It's not easy to get going again because the spiky thoughts will try to block your way. Your mind will be telling you things like "I won't enjoy it" and "I'll make a fool of myself". These thoughts can stop you from trying things out. CBT will help you catch these thoughts and learn to challenge them.

An activity planner is a record of the things you do each day. This will help you and your therapist see the links between what you do and how you feel. You can then use it to spot gaps of time which you can use for fun activities, and things that will give you a sense of having done something worthwhile. It's important you have time for both types of activities – fun ones and ones that help you feel good about yourself.

21/05/04	Activity Planner
.	Went to school.
.	played football with friends.
.	went to swimming pool
.	Came home, did geography homework
.	helped my sister's homework
.	watched the Simpsons.
.	ate chocolate ice cream.
.	read harry potter

Sort your thoughts

We'll call thoughts which make us feel depressed **spiky thoughts** because they are unhelpful; they spike us by making us feel depressed. Thoughts that make us feel better are called **smooth thoughts** because they are more helpful; they help us deal with situations and feel good.

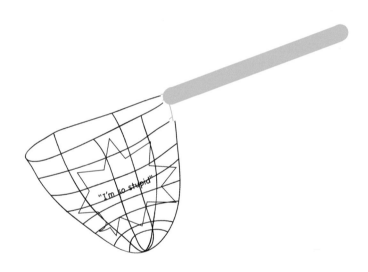

Catching spiky thoughts

Getting to spot spiky thoughts is the first way to overcome them.
This can be difficult, but if you can begin to spot your thoughts,
you are well on your way to work out which ones are spiky
(and make you feel worse) and which ones are smooth (and
make you feel better). Let's look at how to catch spiky thoughts
and question them to get smooth thoughts and feel better.

Situation	Feeling	Spiky thought	What I did
Mum asked me to get some milk when I was at the shop. I forgot.	Terrible, low, guilty	I'm so stupid. I'm a total failure. I can't do anything right.	Went upstairs and hid away in my room from mum.

diary can be downloaded from www.oxdev.co.uk

Spiky thoughts often tell you bad things about yourself, other people and the future. Thought catching takes a bit of practice. You might have some spiky thoughts about how difficult it is at the beginning. However, most people usually find it gets easier with a bit of practice. Noticing a sudden change in how you're feeling can be a good clue that you've just had a spiky thought.

These questions might help you catch the spiky thoughts:

- What was going through my mind just before I began to feel this way?
- What does this say about me, my life, my future?
- What am I afraid might happen?
- What does this mean about how the other person might feel about me?
- What does this situation say to me about other people in general?

Try to trap your thoughts and feelings onto paper as soon as they happen. This isn't always possible, so you may need to make a mental note of it and write it down as soon as you can.

"I'm so stupid"

Looking for evidence: Can I think about this differently?

After you have caught the spiky thought, the next step is to question it carefully. You may find there is a different way of looking at the situation which can change the way you feel. To do this, you need to find out what evidence there is to support the spiky thought, and what evidence there is against it. This evidence will help you question your thought – is it really as spiky as you thought it was? It might sound a bit confusing at first, but a bit of practice and following the steps below will get you going.

1. Start by writing down all the reasons (evidence for) which you think support the spiky thought.

2. Get together the evidence against the spiky thought being true all of the time. These questions might help you get the hang of this part:

The '**best mate**' question: How would someone else I respect think about this situation? What would they say to me?

The '**last time**' question: What actually happened the last time I was in this situation?

The '**hard time**' question: Am I giving myself a hard time? Is this really my fault, or are there other reasons for what has happened?

The '**time travel**' question: If I travelled in time 3 years ahead, how would I look at it?

The '**tunnel vision**' question: Am I ignoring things that are going well?

The '**mind reading**' question: Am I assuming I know what other people are thinking without actually finding out?

Weighing it up

After we have collected all this evidence, we need to weigh it all up. Is there another way of looking at the situation which does not feel as spiky?

Situation	Feeling	Spiky thought	Evidence for	Evidence against	Smooth thought
Mum asked me to get some milk when I was at the shop. I forgot.	Terrible, low, guilty	I'm so stupid. I'm a total failure. I can't do anything right.	I forgot the milk	I remembered the bread and newspaper she wanted. My group liked my part of our science project.	Just because I forgot the milk doesn't mean I'm a total failure. Everyone forgets stuff sometimes.

Weighing up the evidence and having smooth thoughts will help you to begin to feel better about yourself, your life and your future. Although it can be hard to look at things differently at first, especially when you are feeling upset, it gets easier with practice. Gradually, it can become automatic. It's a bit like learning to swim; you have to think about it carefully when you're learning, but then you can jump in and swim off!

Testing it out

Sometimes even though you argue against your spiky thoughts they still hang around. For example, people with depression sometimes expect situations to go wrong, so they don't bother trying to have a good time. This stops them from really testing out whether they could have enjoyed themselves or not.

The best way to tackle stubborn spiky thoughts is to test them out for yourself and see what actually happens.

1. **The prediction** - place your bets! Write down what you think will happen in the situation, how others might behave or what you might do.

2. **The test** - How can you find out whether this will happen? Find a way to test your prediction.

3. **The results** - What actually happened? Did the prediction come true? Did anything happen that gave you more evidence about the spiky thought?

Let's look at this example:

Michaela has been invited to a party. She doesn't want to go because she believes it will be terrible as she will have no one to talk to and nothing to say.

1. **The prediction**: If I go, no one will talk to me and I will be left on my own and will feel awful.

2. **The test**: Go and see what happens. Talk to the people I know, especially at the beginning. Try to smile and look like I am enjoying myself.

3. **The results**: I didn't enjoy it. I felt I had nothing interesting to say. However, people that I knew did talk to me and I wasn't left on my own. My prediction did not come true. Although I felt uncomfortable while I was there, people did talk to me and I am glad I went.

When you've tested out your prediction you can use the results to help you question your spiky thoughts on the spiky thought record we covered earlier.

Preparing for the future

Sometimes people find that after things start getting better, they have a bad patch where it feels like they are right back where they started, down the plughole. At these times, it is really important to remember that you have learnt skills that helped you climb out of the plughole once, so you'll be able to climb out again.

Once you have learnt CBT skills, they do need to be practiced on a regular basis so you can keep doing them well. You might be surprised how the things you've learnt will help you out in lots of different situations in the future.

Finding a therapist

Your General Practitioner (GP) should direct you towards local services where therapy is available free, as part of the NHS. There are also organizations that offer CBT on a private basis, in which case therapy would need to be paid for. You have the right to ask about your therapist's qualifications, change therapists if you are unhappy and to check that your therapist is registered with a professional organization, such as the British Psychological Society (BPS).

With CBT, the overall monitoring and accreditation organization is the British Association of Behavioural and Cognitive Psychotherapies (BABCP). The address for the BABCP is:

BABCP
PO Box 9
Accrington
BB5 0XB

info@babcp.com
Tel 01254 875277

Further information

'So young, so sad, so listen'
By Philip Graham & Carol Hughes
Available from the Royal College of Psychiatrists
Tel 020 7235 2351

www.youngminds.org.uk
An organization for young people, their parents and
professionals concerned about young people's mental health.

www.bullying.co.uk
For people who have been bullied

www.childline.org.uk
For children in trouble or danger
Tel 0800 1111

www.samaritans.org.uk
Samaritans: 08457 909090
jo@samaritans.org

Parents' Information Service
0800 018 2138

Index

Can you help us please?

This is a short questionnaire to help us find out what kind of people read this book, and more importantly, which parts were helpful and which were not so helpful.

Please answer the questions as best you can and return the form to: Blue Stallion Publications, 8a Market Square, Witney, OX28 6BB by post, or complete the online questionnaire at: www.oxdev.co.uk

We assure you that we will deal strictly confidentially with all given information. That means that we would never release any personal information to a third party. We will only use the information to evaluate and improve the books.

How old are you? ☐ years
Are you male or female?   Male ☐   Female ☐
Who do you live with?   Mum ☐   Dad ☐
    Brothers, how many ☐
    Sisters, how many ☐
    Grandparents ☐
    Other ☐

What made you read the book?

Who recommended this book to you?

Who did you read it with?
By yourself ☐
With a parent(s) ☐
With a doctor/therapist ☐
With someone else ☐

Have you ever been to see a therapist/psychologist to help with your
difficulties?   Yes ☐   No ☐

Did the book make therapy any easier for you?
                          Yes ☐   No ☐
              No difference ☐

How helpful have you found this book?
Please mark on the scale below.

| 1 | 2 | 3 | 4 | 5 |

| Not at all helpful | Not that helpful | Quite helpful | Very helpful | Extremely Helpful |

Did you find it easy to understand?

| 1 | 2 | 3 | 4 | 5 |

| Extremely easy to understand | Mostly easy to under-stand | Some easy parts, some difficult to understand | Quite difficult to understand | Very difficult to understand |

What was the most helpful thing you learned from this book?

Was there anything you didn't like about the book?

Would you recommend this book to someone else who had
difficulties?   Yes ☐   No ☐

Please add anything else that you think might be helpful for us to know.

Thank you for your information!

The Publisher